The Many Colors of My Heart

Eddie Sullivan

The Rain and the Sun Publishing—Honesdale, PA
Paperback ISBN: 979-8-9890668-0-3
Hardcover ISBN: 979-8-9890668-1-0
eBook ISBN: 979-8-9890668-2-7
Library of Congress Control Number: 2023916684
Title: *The Many Colors of My Heart*
Author: Eddie Sullivan
Digital distribution | 2023
Hardcover | 2023
Paperback | 2023

Dedication

Nancy,

I'd be lost without you,
Like a sail with no wind
A dreamer without a dream

You are my answered prayer
My light in the dark
The purpose of my life

All that I do
I do for you
With all my love

Table of Contents

The Many Colors of My Heart

The many colors of my heart pour out of me
Like a rainbow painted upon a powdered sky
For all my emotions dance like droplets in oceans
Seas of blue that can never run dry

And the rivers that rush to golden shores
Don't always deliver dazzling displays
Silent moments the world ignores
When the pretty shades turn to browns and grays

Crimson dawn fades to lavender dusk
And as sure as my sun sets, it will again rise
And though at times, I see sapphire skies
Charcoal clouds always return to blind my eyes

Now and then, my heart embodies a fiery beast
Boiling over in ruby red rivers of rage
Then suddenly, it stands as still as a pond without ripples
And soothes as softly as the scents of jasmine and sage

My heart can set a maelstrom of madness into motion
Or whisper as quietly as a summer stillness without a breath
But in darkness deep this heart will weep a sea of blues
With the failing hope of twilight's depth

But then, with a single encouraging word
This heart of mine will shine like silver once again
For in daylight's laughter I play in emerald pastures
Until the blackness of sorrow drains the life from my pen

This ocean in me can certainly be a mysterious riddle
What color below will rise and flow from the oceans inside?
But upon the gilded pages, somewhere in the middle
Is where the many colors of my heart reside

The Lighthouse

I sometimes feel as frightened
As a flower in winter's frost
Like a novel without a story
The meaning in my life becomes lost

I am trampled into dust
By a cause I cannot understand
A hollow heart that's been crushed
White flag held in hand

But with a voice so soft and so soothing
You calm the raging river
And with a touch so gently moving
From the deep, I am delivered

For you have become the beating of my heart
The love that rescues sinking ships
In an ocean without a drop to drink
Salvation's kiss upon blistering lips

You've come to be the song of my soul
The open window beyond closing doors
In a sea besieged by the death of dreams
The lighthouse upon these rocky shores

The Warmth of June

I met you in the warmth of June
And passion's flames set our hearts on fire
We made love in the summer sun
Young lovers filled with burning desire

Oh, that magic of infatuation
Romantic sweethearts with stars in our eyes
We surrendered to every sweet temptation
Without a single cloud in those August skies

We held on through October's rain
When passion cooled like the autumn breeze
It's so strange how it started to change
Like the red and gold of those falling leaves

The fear was planted in the sudden chill
As the seeds of doubt found a place to grow
Would our love endure beyond the fading light?
Or fade from sight in the coming snow?

We crumbled on a November night
When a bitter reality settled in
As we longed for that summer passion
Would our love survive December's wind?

We searched in vain for the warmth of June
When our love used to be so wild and free
But it felt as though the winter gloom
Turned a roaring fire into a February freeze

But then, a kiss of life dawned on an April day
As the melting snows brought a breath of spring
And like blooming marigolds in the month of May
We hold the hope the warmth of June can bring

My Soft Summer Breeze

Upon a canvas of cloudy skies
There's still a rainbow for her to paint
For she's a spirit full of goodness and grace
And we're mere mortals amongst a living saint

And that spirit lights the darkest of nights
Like a glowing candle's gentle flame
And when hardened hearts turn cold as ice
She'll stay a day in the month of May

She'll summon the smile of a summer's meadow
When the winter snows unleash a freeze
Ever she warms me with her life-giving love
For no cold can cool my soft summer breeze

And that love thrives like rays of hope
Heaven's light upon me, glory streaming down
For a radiant beauty emanates from her
A halo floating above, an angel's holy crown

And the load upon her shoulders
Is more than anyone should have to bear
Still, she shines in shimmering moonlight
My ballerina dancing on air

And sparkles flash in those loving eyes
As her laughter whispers between the trees
She's the bright white in my denim blue skies
My blanket in winter, my soft summer breeze

A Grandfather's Lullaby

I feel it slipping away somehow
More of life passed, than ahead now
Less to look forward to, I find I'm looking behind
And all I have seen in others
Generations of fathers and mothers, sisters and brothers
Now reside in this aging mind slowly in decline

But at least I look back with no regrets
The love that sustains still remains what one never forgets
And it has made this life worthwhile
One day I'll smile when they say goodbye
For now, the young ones gather around
The old storybook they have found
I impart tales of adventure as wide as the sky
And rock them to sleep with a grandfather's lullaby

Once forever young, I feel it coming undone
Never thought an outdated song didn't belong
But no steady beat guides these worn-out feet
At any rate, I'd give anything to stand up straight
Everything's changed, their dance seems so strange
An empty stage, the final page
And like friends long gone, I await a similar fate

An hourglass running out of sands
Final plans now in their hands
I just hope to leave behind something to be remembered by
But for now, I need to rest
For every little test leaves me out of breath
So let me find comfort
As they sing me an old snappy number
And rock me to sleep with a grandfather's lullaby

Never Time Enough

The sunlight is failing in this home you've made
As my soft summer breeze begins to fade
So little time for us, my love
A lifetime of memories—never time enough

Your sparkling eyes, the stars cannot replace
The last light of a smile on your beautiful face
So little time to shine, my love
A lifetime of memories—never time enough

Our paradise grows dim, like a weeping sunset
Your laughter withers beneath my song of regret
I'll shatter like glass when you're no longer here
Every dream, in the shadow of a mournful tear

Mere moments to dance beneath the moon
Our tango together ending much too soon
How swiftly they flow, these sands of time
Oh, stay one moment more, lady love of mine

Growing shorter, each shallow breath
Each heartbeat whispers of tears to be wept
The creeping coldness of a November night
No picnics in the park in life's dwindling light

Nightfall approaches, eyes soon to close
I feel the anguish a loving heart only knows
And I pray that angels at Heaven's gate
Reach out holy hands as they wait

And so, I let you go
Goodbye, my love
This lifetime together….
Never time enough

Time Stands Still

Quiet, sits the schoolyard where we once played
Lonely, lies the home where I once lived
And though tracks of tears take time to fade
This offer of comfort is all I can give

The sword of sorrow has pierced you deeply
And your pain casts a shadow you cannot shake
Grief forges a blade that cuts completely
And loneliness, an anchor with immeasurable weight

But our faith fosters a light in our darkest hour
And hope bestows a beacon in the deepest abyss
And love lives on where death has no power
And no belief can be greater than this

I now live again in a paradise unseen
Where angels sing melodies born of a dream
I dance like a child with wings on her feet
In bright green meadows and gold-covered streets

So look to the skies for my beautiful face
Listen for my voice in a song of celebration
In this heavenly home, this glorious place
Where every soul becomes a new creation

My joy is whispered with every breath
My sparkling eyes shine like the sun
I'll be waiting for you where the heart is kept
For time stands still when you're forever young

The Pages of the Panoramic Past

The panoramic past
The pages of our memories
A glimpse of yesterday's joy
Within the wake of tragedies

Like photos you cannot erase
From a soul's wandering mind
Their once upon a times
Can not be left behind

For the return of endless smiles
Of those so most beloved
Will surely forever remain
What we most desire and covet

And though their images linger
Where their love first cast a shadow
The eyes of the heart are timeless
And their love shall always follow

Majestic

Majestic, you fly above the mountains
Carrying the spirits of millennia past
The wisdom of ages rides on your wingtips
The hope of freedom is held in your hands

I stand in awe of your effortless wind dance
Watching the movements you make with no sound
Majestic, I wonder are you there to guide me
To the place where all my answers are found?

Majestic, you fly down into the valley
Carrying with you the meaning of life
All that our fathers released with their last breath
Rides with you in your glorious flight

And I'm just a man in search of himself
Your walk on the wind gives life to my song
But you know where to go without even searching
For where you are is where you belong

Majestic, you fly through an ocean of blue sky
To lands unknown, horizons unseen
Perhaps one day I'll ride by your side
To worlds that live beyond all my dreams

Majestic, you fly straight into the heavens
A picture of perfection in a sky everlasting
Majestic, please let me learn from you lessons
Teach me to fly into a life never passing

Whispering Wind

The words still echo through a heart abandoned
Like a whispering wind through a bottomless canyon
The water-colored portrait still runs in the rain
And the tracks of her tears still follow the train

Time never surrenders the sorrow of separation
No hope can ease her soul's desperation
The heartbreaking image of goodbye never fades
And teardrops on a page leave lasting stains

The lingering shadows of an impassioned kiss
The last drops of a heart's departing bliss
As billows of smoke rise in her mind
No memory of mercy in foreboding skies

The anger of Heaven was felt in the ground
And in angels' tears, the sky was drowned
Her smile washed away into a raging river
And a soaking sadness, the day delivered

Anguish upon a young woman's face
As pain pierced their final embrace
Until it came undone with a tap on his shoulder
And her hell-bound soldier could no longer hold her

"Will you wait for me?" the last words he spoke
A solemn swear, a prayer to invoke
And with the lingering taste of one last kiss
The words still chase the whispering wind

A World Away

Seeking solace in her secret sanctuary
She recalls her childhood days
Through a Valentine's card from a six year old
He calls out to her from a world away

Melancholy melodies, she plays on her piano
In her private world with the curtains closed
A silver picture frame captures his smile
A book of memories her heart only knows

No words to be heard
Through the solitude of sorrow's surrender
Coffee cups piling up
And scattered dinner plates force her to remember

The world goes on for the rest
Amidst soul-stirring images from a world away
A soldier's uniform neatly pressed
A train bound for a rainy day

The boy with the baby blue eyes
And the smile that set her on fire
Memories of a moonlit kiss
Sweetest breath of young desire

Yet, fear accompanies each knock on her door
Echoes of promises—hard to keep, easy to say
A sorrowful soul strikes a somber chord
Until the boy she loves returns
From a hell on Earth a world away

A Star Falls in the West

In the shadow of Rome
A Mediterranean breeze sighs upon lavender silk
And the curtains part to reveal a black velvet canopy
And a night of a trillion skies
Draped in scarlet satin
Stands a bride clothed in youth and stunning beauty
She stares into the night
With starlight twinkling in her deep ebony eyes

Freshly-christened love awaits
In a bed of rose-colored passion and rich red wine
Little did he know, however
She had become a woman
Long before she had ever become his bride....

The secret only one other shares
Lays sleeping where the ocean rushes to familiar shores
Love destined from ages past wears no chains
And across wide spaces and eternity gone by
That once in a lifetime still endures
Eternally, his touch lingers
Entrenched in a heart that never wanted to relinquish it
A girl who gave him her childhood
The boy whose passion ignited hers
And nothing in the world can extinguish it

Here, after all these years gone by
Partially at peace, yet unable to rest
Wondering why, she gazes at the Roman sky
Just as a star falls in the west

Guardian Angels

Sleep, little darling
As I sing sweet dreams to you tonight
And may your guardian angel watch over you
As you rest your curious eyes

Lose yourself in your world of wonder
And rest assured I will always keep you safe
For love brought to life my precious treasure
Who fills my heart with redeeming grace

Sleep in peace, my babe
For peace is what you bring to my soul
And as I watch the rhythm of your breaths
I watch the wisdom of Heaven unfold

You have saved a lost and lonely life
My wings were broken before you were born
But somehow, someone somewhere knew
And from stardust and moonbeams you were formed

So dream, little one, of lands far away
Of princes and princesses long ago
Know that I watch over you today
And I know, you'll watch over me tomorrow

For I live to be your guardian angel
To sing you softly to sleep with a soothing lullaby
I'll be your guardian angel until the end of time
And you, sweet child….will always be mine

Far Beyond the Sounds of the City

Far beyond the sounds of the city
    She hears her heart longing for home
    For no blossoms bloom in concrete gardens
And when the earth hardens
No rose is grown in solid stone

One in a sea of endless faces
No traces of the easy breeze she once wore
Lost amidst disappointment's kiss
The light in his eyes now only rise
As a blue horizon on some celestial shore

The promise of a life's worth of love
Sealed within a sacred ceremony of blissful dreams
But beneath the city's thunder
There lies no wonder in a bucket full of teardrops
And a soul cannot breathe without the air it needs

Through it all, serenity beckons
Where the heavenly hills reach with their flowering trees
The place she had sorely missed
And the lips she hadn't kissed for far too long
Wait patiently with the sweetest song
And sweet dreams between mountain streams

Open arms await at the station
With a cup overflowing with serenity's salvation
And as she breathes in their embrace
She opens to love like lilies in spring
And finally, far beyond the sounds of the city
Her heart can hear the sweet songs she longs to sing

Forever Hold Your Peace

Nervous bride paces beneath bells beckoning
As fate decides whether to render a reckoning
And melodic tones from an organ's pipes
Enhance an atmosphere both joyous and foreboding
Uncertain groom searches feelings
Beneath saints painted on ceilings
Radiant smiles on both sides of the aisles
But could the ever after already be eroding?

Well-dressed guests, eager anticipation
Impending nuptuals, subsequent celebration
The best man holds two rings of gold
A flower girl's petals on Italian tile
A letter from the past unwittingly haunting
A final decision ever so daunting
Sleeps in a dreamer with a deadly secret
And a past no demon could ever reconcile

She graces the awestruck congregation
With an angelic gown at its destination
All eyes fix upon this vision of perfection
But in one soul lurks a storm of tears
The bouquet rests in the maid of honor's hands
The lifting of the veil reveals sunlit strands
But a truth lives to tell a story hushed
Buried in the dust for eternity's years

The words commence, so often spoken
But is one heart about to be broken?
The congregation awaits
As the captive contemplates a liberating release
Hearts pounding, echoes resounding
"Speak now," says the priest, "or forever hold your peace."

The Fruit of My Vine

My sun rises through the light in your eyes
My life begins when I'm wrapped in your arms
Birds do not sing until they hear your sweet voice
For joy is felt only wherever you are

But being apart feels like winter's lament
Love's fire cannot burn when the heart has no spark
No light can shine through night's moonless sky
No hope for my dreams when I'm lost in the dark

Without you near, no food for my soul
For only you can soothe my deepest need
With miles between, an insatiable thirst
For the fruit of my vine—so rich and so sweet

Away from your love, no breath is left
I'm a desperate dreamer, gasping for air
Praying for a dance, but a chorus of sighs
A heart with no home, no promise in prayer

My hunger for living—only one flavor
My thirst for love—only one wine
For your presence is nectar, heavenly sent
The harvest is blessed, the fruit of my vine

In your loving arms my heart has a home
For you are my essence, the very air I breathe
In your eyes live my dreams, and promise fulfilled
You're the fruit of my vine—so rich and so sweet

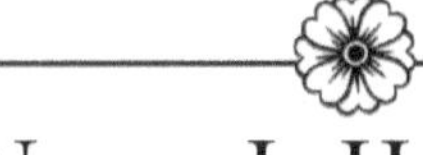

Nancy Is Her Name

Nancy is her name
The girl who sits there in the park
Day after day
From noon until one o'clock
I asked her for her name
And could I sit down next to her
We fell in love right away
Now things are like they never were....

Nancy is her name
Or at least, perhaps it could be
It's the name that I gave
To the one who took my heart from me
I'm going over there, this time
And what a lucky guy I'll be
I'll look into her eyes
And her love will be looking back at me....

Nancy was her name
Or at least, perhaps it could've been
I can't forget that day
She met a handsome gentleman
She looked into his eyes
And never did come back again
Now, he's the lucky guy
And I wish it was me instead of him....

Nancy was her name
She never knew I loved her
But I love her still the same
Even though I never knew her
I remember still today
The girl who sat there in the park
The one who got away
I still see her there in my heart

Echoes in the Night

Once, I felt the magic of Eden
A love that led where joy could follow
Once, I kissed a magical maiden
Beneath a waterfall in an enchanted hollow

In her eyes, I saw Heaven's gate
In her hair, a field of gold
In her kiss, I felt a life-giving breath
In her heart, a treasure to behold

But was the breath that brought my passion to life
Nothing more than echoes in the night?

Once, we played in a pleasurable paradise
Where a glorious truth lived in a fairytale
Once, we rode a promising wave
Where a westerly wind filled an eager sail

In our hands, we held Heaven's key
In our grasp, the Earth and sky
In my heart, dwelled a beautiful peace
In my soul, a soothing lullaby

But when I awoke in the real world below
I heard the sounds of laughter echo
For the vision of paradise I'd been shown
Was only reality's hopeful shadow

And the treasure I found in that field of gold
Brought a dream that died in the morning light
And the tale of magic the sleeper had been told
Turned out to be nothing more than echoes in the night

The Starry Eyes of Strangers

The starry eyes of strangers
Met from across the way
The princely man of the world
And the girl of a summer's day
They were swept away in an instant
Embers, destined to ignite
Indeed, as the saying goes
It was truly, love at first sight

Families, friends, and neighbors
Traveled hundreds of miles
To toast this happy marriage
With fine champagne and smiles
They made their hopeful wishes
With cordial kisses and laughter
For the new bride and groom
To love forever after

With a promising future foretold
By fools dressed as sages
It was proclaimed their love would become
A fabled one for the ages
And though the fairytale romance
Was bound with gilded seams
It is between the lines
Only a wise one reads

For what is never written
In the book of love's pages
Is that a wild, wandering heart
Is never capable of changes
For one's lustful desires
Are not the same as one's needs
And the one left behind is always
The one left dangling in the breeze

Blinded Heart

Deep in my soul I know
A kiss from your lips is deadly
But the heart of this fool is always
Too blind to see you killing me
Common sense has tried to tell me
That with all the heartache you've brought
This blinded heart should've learned
The painful lessons you've taught

But your grip of empty promises
And seduction I cannot escape
Silence the voices of reason
That warn me of my fate

Despite the sound advice
Of friends who all mean well
My pain still chooses to remain
In this heart's unholy hell
And though a wise one lives within
Who knows the simple truth
I'm blind to the knives in your eyes
That show me living proof

For my blinded heart looks past
All the wrong that's been done
It sits and waits for more
When a wise one would get up and run
My heart is blind to the pain
As I let you reign over me
And this foolish romantic loves
What my blinded heart will never
Allow itself to see

Until It Fades

I found you in the morning light
And our love blossomed like a newborn rose
We danced in the garden of paradise
Where the sun's always warm, and new love grows
But I treated you like a discarded treasure
And went off to play in foreign lands
I gave you pain, while I took your pleasure
And the one true love slipped through my hands

You held my heart like a holy chalice
You poured out your love like sacred wine
But an evil weed spread throughout the palace
Where the light of perfect beauty shines
You were warm and true, and always faithful
A life of love awaited me
But my lust for the fruit of another table
Drove a demon to the dark who hated me

You're the one I never will forget
I just never saw the sun until it set
A fool destroys all that love creates
I never know what I have until it fades
The golden heart that heaven made
Was the precious gift I threw away
You were one in a million, weren't you, babe?
But I never see the light until it fades

Lonely People

Lonely people, in lonely bedrooms
Listen now for the faint whisper of hope from above
A voice of compassion softly speaks within the silence
A love song written in your name waits to be sung

Lonely people, lost in the darkness
Look for the room upstairs where the light is always on
I know the night wields a wicked sword
But when you look to where the sun rises
You'll forever find the dawn

Lonely people, through endless winters
A golden meadow lies in store at a rainbow's end
Beyond the cold, comfort is given
As hurting souls are wrapped in the warmth of a timeless friend

Lonely people, in torrents of teardrops
Your cries of sadness are heard by Heaven's heart
And though your prayers don't seem to get answered
Angels watch over the lonely
As the lonely watch for a falling star

Lonely people, longing for love
For every someone, there's someone somewhere who cares
I promise that soon azaleas will bloom
And all the love the lonely long for
Will, at last, be theirs

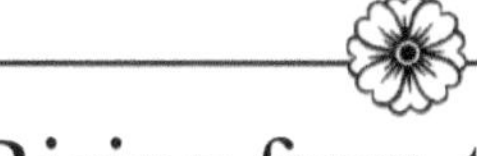

Rising from the Ashes

Your epic tale of romance
Was written like a storybook fantasy
Where your happy-ever-after paradise
Lived far beyond reality

The prince of your heart loved you
In your dream world of fairy-tale loves
Where the flames of passion burned
With the heat of a thousand suns

But your castle walls crumbled
Like a kingdom of make believe
And those passionate flames dwindled
Like the light of a winter's eve

You portrayed an innocent princess
A lily once open to trust
Now you search for remnants of romance
Amongst embers turned to dust

Gone, is that prince who loved you
Not so long ago
And the lily has lost the dream
With which she needs to grow

But be assured that real love
Is a dream that still exists
It just doesn't include the perfection
Of a little girl's magical prince

So the time has come to learn
Fairy-tale lovers are pretending
And only a storybook fantasy
Provides the perfect ending

But love will bestow a new dream
Upon every soul who tries
And from the ashes of heartbreak
Once more, your heart will rise

Come in from the Storm

Can you come in from the storm?
From the things they've said that haunt you in the night?
Can you move on from the past?
Leave the dark behind, and move into the light?
Can you wipe away the tears?
All the words that cut straight into your heart?
Can you forgive the ones hurting you
For all the wounds, all the bruises, all the scars?

Can the child live in you
Who is seeing through their sins of yesterday?
Can you let your heart forget?
Through your weeping eyes, can you love them anyway?
Can you open the door?
Because holding on becomes a prison without a key
Can you tell the ones hurting you
That from all you've said and all you've done
I'm setting myself free?

Let it go, let it out
Because it will make you lose your mind
Let it be, set it free
Let the healing give you life

Because there's freedom in forgiveness
That will heal a wounded heart
There's a joy in absolution
That will fill the deepest scars
There's a harbor waiting for you
When you come in from the storm
Let the light of love restore your soul
And make your way back home

My Misty Blue Eyes

Many times I need to hide
The doubts and fears I feel
For I've suffered many scars inside
That my heart chooses to conceal
There's a reason I keep them hidden
Behind my misty blue eyes
And if you search the shadowy corners
You'll be shocked by what you find

My book's colorful cover
Is all I allow you to see
Some pages have lines too deep
For the faint of heart to read
I only reveal the rainbows
In the pictures in between
While the haunted demons within
Remain the pages unseen

For some secluded secrets
Are simply meant to be kept
Insecurities that lie at the bottom
Of this ocean's darkest depth
For the truth is a troubling tale
Left to the author to tell
Some emotions aren't for sale
They're just too private to sell

I sprinkle sugary stories
Of the lighthearted brightness of day
But beware the shaded colors
In the shadows of dazzling displays
For the tears behind my smiles
Don't ride on the wings of butterflies
Inside, lives a frightened child
Behind my misty blue eyes

World of Dreams

A world of dreams
Locks that seem to have no keys
A world of possibilities only a hopeful heart sees
Yet, through a thousand frustrated lifetimes
With no combination of reasons and rhymes
Here, on bended knees
Still, it calls out to me

And I can't let it go
Although I know the riddle remains reclusive
The prayer to getting there, ever elusive
Season after season, for whatever reason, I can't stop climbing
And down that slope, there goes my hope
And I can't keep myself from sliding

I brush myself off anyway
No matter what the critics say
My dreams—they sink to the bottom and rust
As I search the wind for salvation amidst the dust
But something unknown, something unshown
Compels me to continue, tells me I must

The key waits for me, patiently
Hiding like some celestial secret in the back of my mind
And like a pirate without a treasure map, the path is black
And the fool is leading the blind

But this captive refuses to remain bound to a chain
Somewhere beyond the mortar and stone lies that world unknown
That world of dreams I'm still trying to find
And though I'm years behind
I choose to continue to chase that sweetest taste
That place only a daring dreamer believes
That world of dreams only my hopeful heart sees

The Child Inside

Surely, no boundaries exist
In worlds a child creates
There lives only an artist within
With a canvas on which to paint
Surely, our horizons encompass
No beginning or end
Only pages that wait for color
From the hand with the brush and the pen

Surely, no walls can stop
The beauty of our minds from flowing
Only endless streams that lead
To where the magic's forever growing
Surely, no chains can bind us
When we roam as an untethered spirit
An unwritten story lives inside us
And only a dreamer can hear it

So, let your imagination
Determine your destination
Let the child inside come alive
In a world of your own creation
For something resides beyond
What aging eyes perceive
The stars we wish upon
The air with which we breathe
So dream your new discoveries
Where the young at heart reside
For endless possibilities
Live within the child inside

Searching

Dying love paints a page of history
Memories with a taste so bittersweet
A whisper of goodbye in the fading light of yesterday
I sit and search the meaning of
Why I was to fall in love
When the smile in your eyes
Was just a fleeting kiss the wind blew away

I wish the answers would speak out loud
Telling me of destiny's purpose
Why do we find the love we dream about
If it's only going to hurt us?
Still...I know time will clear my mind
The passion lost, I'll leave behind
For the heavens hold the love my hurting heart hopes to find
And so, I'm searching…searching one more time

I look back on the tracks of tears
As the shroud of sadness slowly disappears
But it's the final raindrops that always leave a lasting stain
I look back on the you-and-me that's gone
I look ahead to the promise of a new day's dawn
And hold on to the hopes for tomorrow's love that still remain

But for now, what I wish for most of all
Is freedom from memory's heartache
A little love through the loneliness
A little light to fill the dark space
Still... it's time to move on from the past
From the shadow of despair you still cast
You were the holder of my heart
But you're not the last my heart will find
And so, I'm searching…searching one more time

Something Got Left Behind

It seems so long ago, when we were close
Childhood memories of you, I cherish most
If I try, I still hear the joyful sounds
Close my eyes, and I still see us at the playground
Oh, how we thought it would never change
But then, I moved a million miles away
And it feels like I've moved to the dark side of the moon
And my friend at the other end is someone I once knew

I left my home, in search of a better place
Headed for the hills, for a world of dreams to chase
Something to call my own, was what I had hoped to find
But somewhere along the road, something got left behind

The way we used to feel when we were young
Playing ball in the warmth of the summer sun
In my dreams, I hear the sounds of laughter
And to this day, it's a sound I still chase after
It's such a mystery how life unravels
So much seems lost on the roads one travels
And we never know what's around the bends
How space can grow between the closest of friends

I left my home, in search of a better place
Climbed a mountain to the world of dreams I chase
Something to call my own, I'm still trying to find
But somewhere along the road, something got left behind
Leaving the fold to go dig for gold
I left the city streets to walk a country road
But on the way to what I'm still hoping to find
A part of me died, and something got left behind

A Flower in the Forest

We look for the light of love
Deep in the darkest forest
We listen for a beating heart
Beneath a clamorous chorus
We hope to see ourselves
In eyes that look into our own
We hope to find a flower
Where none has ever gown

We forage for fertile soil
Amongst the endless trees
We search for open land
To plant our delicate seeds
We envision a lasting lover
In the silhouette of a stranger
But are blinded by painted colors
And the artificial flavor

For although a box of chocolates
Holds tempting, seductive sweets
We all need food from the field
For a flower to find what it needs
We look for our better half
In the mirrors of our minds
And sometimes what one seeks
Is sometimes what one finds

For I, too, was a wanderer
Through a forest of many faces
Entangled in thorns and thickets
Longing for open spaces
Until that one seed I planted
Found a good place to grow
And the beautiful flower I cared for
Found my heart as its home

The Moment Your Eyes Met Mine

Around the block a time or two
To places I did not belong
I've fallen hard and I've fallen through
With all the ones who were all wrong

And I've been fooled more than once
By the thrill of passion's fire
But I need more than another's touch
To fulfill my heart's desire

I have learned my lesson well
Infatuation and true love
Comes a time when you can tell
The right one has finally come

I have searched long and hard
For the love we hope to find
My search came to an end
The moment your eyes met mine

He Loved Only Once

He loved only once, and never again
    She, and no other
    No matter where, no matter when
He loved her, there and then
Once, but never again

Emotions, no conceivable words can express
Desire—never the more
But those memories linger nevertheless
And since destiny would never impart upon him
His forever and a day
That one frozen moment in time will forever remain
His once in a lifetime his heart will never let fade away

And no gold or silver shall ever again shine
For she—that one love, truly divine
Rendered his eternal soul eternally blind
Indeed, she embodied a breathless beauty
Unlike any his eyes had ever seen
She became his one flawless diamond
Perfection's timeless dream

An angelic smile he could never forget
Upon his captive heart, permanently etched
Her incredible dark eyes so deeply bewitching
As black as the stars' underlying canopy
But the starlight flashed just a fleeting glimpse
Of the only skies his eyes would ever desire to see
And still, that goddess-like vision forever remains
In his dreamworld, where the queen of his heart forever reigns

And he loved her, there and then
Once, but never again
No matter what was to come
Or whatever had passed
He loved only once, and forever the last

The King Comes Crashing Down

Once upon a mountain high
I hitched a ride on an eagle's wings
I soared through the heavens like a shooting star
And saw the place where angels sing
My queen was adorned with a golden crown
In our paradise of pure delights
Songs of angels filled the air
And carried our hearts to endless heights

But a fool fumbles a fortune found
And a careless king comes crashing down

Once in dreamer's fantasy
I held my world like sand in my hands
I laughed when fate was warning me
Laughed at all of karma's plans
My queen smiled down from her golden throne
And we cast our cares to the wind
We never thought they'd find us there
Never saw the fall begin

But then, I stumbled on a stepping stone
And fell from grace with a thunderous sound
All our gold has been squandered and sold
To Earth, the king comes crashing down
And now, it's time to face reality
The fool in the fantasy has been found
The reaper knocks upon my door
And to Earth, the king comes crashing down

Speak Softly

Please lay beside me upon our pillows
For worry weighs heavy upon my weary soul
My world falls apart within our windows
And there's so much of it I cannot control
I need your comfort, like I need to breathe
For the questions of tomorrow spin a whirlwind within
And the mistakes of yesterday for which I grieve
Leave me not knowing where to begin

My beloved, please quiet this tormented mind
And tell me this endless winter is going to end
That I'll be safe from the past from which I hide
And we'll win the future we fight to defend
I need your reassurance again
For sometimes I lose my sense of worth
I suffer from wondering why and when
And sometimes it seems such a fruitless search

So speak softly, my love, with the tenderness of an angel
Whisper sweetness into my ear
For I hurt like a child with wounds so painful
And only you can make the darkness disappear
So speak softly, my love, and tell me you love me
For much too easily I give in to fear
But for you to say you'll never leave me
Is all the hope I'll need to hear

Silver Lining

The weight of the whole world is on your shoulders
And all you can think of is all of your troubles
There's a leprechaun handing out three-leaf clovers
And he keeps bursting all of your bubbles

Your laughter lies buried beneath a pile of problems
And your smile stays covered with a veil of tears
You think you see a lighthouse out in the distance
But then, the shelter of the shoreline disappears

But there's a silver lining in there, I swear
There's a rainbow at the end of all of this somewhere

The tide of despair is pulling you under
You're lost in a sea of stormy emotion
And there's a dark cloud rolling with thunder
As you drown alone in this endless ocean

Your laughter lies buried beneath a blizzard of heartache
And your smile is smothered with a veil of tears
You see an oasis out in the distance
But then, the water in the desert disappears

But there's a silver lining in there, I swear
A rainbow awaits at the end of this, somewhere
A reason remains for all the seasons of life
And somewhere beyond all the darkness, there's light

There's a child deep inside us, wearing a smile
A cause for celebration, once in a while
There's a playground nearby full of laughter and joy
And beneath our pile of problems
Lives a happy little girl, a happy little boy

The Rain and the Sun

If I am the stone wall that crumbles and cracks
Then you are the mason putting my pieces back
My desire is an ocean engulfed by a storm
And your love is a fire all cozy and warm

There's a madman inside me who loses control
And you are the therapy soothing my soul
For I am a fool with a will made of stone
And you are the healer who fills all the holes

And I need you beside me
To enlighten and guide me
Through the clouds and the haze
Of life's endless maze

For you and I go together like the rain and the sun
Destined for each other since the world was begun
Two parts of the same soul, together as one
United forever, until all time is done

And I need you beside me
To enlighten and guide me
Through the clouds and the haze
Of life's endless maze

For you are the candle
Aglow in the window
You are the warm wind
That brings me back home

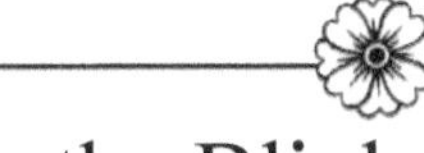

In the Blink of an Eye

Three days ago, I was a child
Or was my childhood just a dream?
Now playing on Dad's home movies
My first day up on the screen
And suddenly, I am awake
In a time and place so far away
At times, it seems another lifetime
At times, it seems like just a day

Two days ago, we fell in love
We took our vows, and made a home
Yesterday the children came along
And through the hours, we watched them grow
And then, today, they said goodbye
Off to find a life of their own
They learned to walk just yesterday
And traveled a thousand miles from home

One by one, we say goodbye to family and friends
As we suddenly turn old and gray
But we can still remember being children
Just like it was yesterday

Just days ago, I came to be
Or was this life of mine just a dream?
Now playing on God's home movies
A lifetime up on the screen

We turn around
And much of life has passed us by
Sometimes it seems life happens
In the blink of an eye
A moment ago
Was a hundred years gone by
And suddenly our lives have passed
In the blink of an eye

Amazingly Beautiful

It's early October
And I'm driving through the countryside
I'm lost in this magical canvas of heavenly delight
Seeing this glorious splendor of grand design
Lets me know there is surely a love divine
The leaves on the trees are reminders to me
How amazingly beautiful this world can be
And I'm sorry, my Lord, for the times I complain
When I'm lost in the misery, lost in the rain
But this breathtaking scene has allowed me to see
How amazingly beautiful this world can be

The long day is over
And I'm heading home to my wife
With a bounty of blessings
Good fortune poured into my life
As I walk through the door I can hardly believe my eyes
This incredible woman is waiting with arms open wide
A smile on her face and I'm living the dream
This amazingly beautiful woman loves me
And I'm sorry, my Lord, for the times I complain
When I lost in the misery, lost in the rain
But when I look in her eyes, it's so easy to see
How amazingly beautiful she is to me

And at times all the good things just fade into blue
When they're buried so deep in the troubles we face
Sometimes we just need a reminder or two
That somewhere in our prayers lies the cup of your grace

I'm lying in bed in this moment of solitude
She's dreaming of sunsets on the shores of June
My overjoyed spirit feels like it's been renewed

So I quietly offer this prayer of my gratitude
This amazingly beautiful light touching me
Is the glory of Heaven that gives my heart peace
And I'm sorry, my Lord, for the times I complain
When I'm lost in the misery, lost in the rain
But it's moments like these that allow me to see
How amazingly beautiful this life can be
Yes, moments like these are reminders to me
How amazingly beautiful…this life can be

Silent River

Another year has passed me by
Like a flash of time in the nighttime sky
Where do our fleeting lives seem to go?
We walk along the shore, and watch the silent river flow
Another moment in an eternity of time
Gone forever, like youth past its prime
The mystery of it all is more than we'll ever know
And long after we're gone, the silent river will silently flow

Another yesterday, like clouds of gray floating by
The past—an ocean deepening, an ever-expanding sky
A mountain of memories in the mirror waving goodbye
And sometimes it's without remorse or romance
The silent river doesn't give any of it a second glance
Another friend has finished their race
Picture on the mantle of their familiar face
While words left to say slip through our hands
We sift through the sands
As the silent river does its silent dance

Another breath—how many left for each of us to take?
So, will we once again, another moment together forsake?
Or will we cherish our treasures while there's still a chance?
While the silent river rushes into the ocean's hands
Another heartbeat—hopefully, many more before daylights fades
The ticking of a clock—a reminder of our numbered days
And though pleasures and pains leave lasting stains
No two lives ever unfold the same—yet, constant, time remains
And still, it's all connected like every wind that blows
And like stardust from the heavens
The silent river forever flows

What If

What if all our dreams came true, like a picture-perfect sky?
What if every day felt like fireworks on the fourth of July?
What if genies came along granting wishes in a flash?
What if we could reach the stars, and all we had to do was ask?
What if you and I could ride a rocket to the moon?
What if we lived in a great big house where joy filled every room?
What if all our troubles came with answers written down?
And what if all we're searching for, suddenly was found?

What if every hungry heart had all they needed to live?
What if those who had too much were more willing to give?
What if everything was fair, and nobody did without?
And what if a single cup of love was enough to go around?
What if every child wore a smile upon their face?
What if no one held an ounce of hate in the whole human race?
What if the world was a perfect place, and peace reigned everywhere?
All our hopes were found right here and now, instead of way out there?

And what if every song I wrote could reach into your soul?
What if every word I spoke became wisdom made of gold?
So, let me put my two cents in, for what it might be worth
Perfection is made in Heaven, never meant for here on Earth
There's a lot of things we'll never own
While in this world we roam
So, I guess we'll all just have to wait
Until the good Lord brings us home

Yes, I guess we'll just have to wait….
Until the good Lord brings us home

After the Storm

Can we pick up the pieces after the storm?
Can we open the shutters, and let in the sun?
All our memories are scattered along the shore
Where the wild horses used to run
Broken hearts, like broken glass
Spread across the floor
Can we sweep these tears away?
And restore these hearts once more?

Here's a picture of lovers who danced in the light
There's a crack in the frame that holds it in place
If we could step back in time to who we were that night
We could recapture the smile upon your face
Where do we turn when hope is lost?
Scattered in the wind?
Can we look into each other's eyes
And find the courage to hope again?

There's a rainbow appearing after the storm
If we open the shutters, and let in the sun
I see a vision of lovers who dance on the shore
And of wild horses who love to run

I don't want to give up on the home of our hearts
There's a solid foundation deep in our souls
All the walls are still standing on the love we still feel
We can pick up the pieces, and patch all the holes
Where there's a will, there's a way, they say
I believe in you, my home
We can find the quiet peacefulness
In the gentle breeze after the storm

A Million Miles Away

The past is like a ghost hiding in the dark
Regret is like a dagger stabbing at the heart
How do we move on from mistakes we have made?
All that's led us here to where we stand today?
Can we stop thinking about what might've been?
The movie plays in our minds, again and again
What happened to the life we thought we would have?
Images of the future, echoes of the past

So, now we find ourselves more than a million miles away
A million miles from where we thought we would be today
But with hope in our hearts, the dream can be ours
So let's take a step today, one step along the way
And the star we follow will be closer tomorrow
Than a million miles away

A billion broken pieces lying on the ground
Two daring dreamers good fortune hasn't found
Longing for something that still isn't ours
Praying for a miracle, wishing on the stars
But there's hope on the horizon, a light in our eyes
Like the morning sun, ready to rise
And if we look ahead, instead of looking behind
I know there's a pot of gold the two of us can find

So, now we find ourselves less than a million miles away
Closer now than where we stood only yesterday
Here we are, closing in, one step at a time
To all we dare to dream, all that's yours and mine
Because we're leaving behind all that has been
We're opening the doors, and running like the wind
There's hope in our hearts, and soon the dream is ours
We'll spread our wings today, and we'll be on our way
And the star we follow will be closer tomorrow
Than a million miles away

Swept Away

When I look into your beautiful eyes
A world of love opens up for me
Like a flower beneath big, blue skies
Swaying in the summer breeze
I'm like a shell swept away from a sandy shore
When your eyes draw me in to an endless sea
I feel the tide pull me overboard
And I get lost in the sweetest dream

Swept away toward the light of day
By the heart that leads me home
I'm swept away

Every word you speak becomes a lullaby
Every sound, as sweet as a robin's song
Voice as soft as an angel's sigh
A whispered breath of dawn
Your smile is the path to Heaven's gate
A day in the park, lying in the sun
I feel like a boy on his first date
A dreamer, forever young

Swept away, like leaves in the wind
You're an open heart, and I'm rushing in
Swept away by the ocean's waves
Lost in the tide, I'm swept away
Swept away to the stars above
I ride the sky on your wings of love
Swept away toward the light of day
By the heart that leads me home
I'm swept away

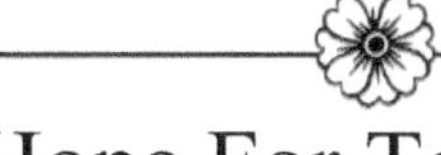

Hope For Tomorrow

Let us not drown
In the wake of yesterday's sin
Let us not lament
Over what could've been
Let us not relive
The old mistakes we have made
Nor hide in the shadows
Of self pity and shame

Live not in the fear
Of repeating the past
Count not the misfortunes
We have amassed
Mourn not for expectations
That have not been met
Fear not the frustrations
That have not come yet

For though we walk between
The dark and the light
Remember the dawn
Always follows the night
So look not to where
Teardrops tend to follow
Let us instead, look ahead
With eyes full of hope for tomorrow

Let us dine at a table divine
Where none of yesterday's sorrow
Comes back today to borrow
Let us instead, look ahead
To where happy hearts
Hold onto hope for tomorrow

Christmas Wish

I was strolling down Main Avenue
With my load of Christmas gifts
When I came upon a young mother
Trying to comfort her two kids
They were staring through the window
Of the children's favorite store
When I sadly heard their mother say,
"Those are things we can't afford."

I saw the tears in those little eyes
And it stopped me in my tracks
I noticed the shoes upon their feet
The old clothes upon their backs
With a gentle touch, I said, "excuse me, ma'am,
I'd like to help you if I could."
I slipped a hundred dollars in her hand
And said, "I hope this does some good."
She looked at me, and began to cry
And said, "God bless you, sir."
And as she hugged her kids, I waved goodbye
And I made this wish for her:
"I hope you get your wish, this Christmas
Whatever it may be
Perhaps a new home of your own
Good health for your family."

After stopping for some coffee
I resumed my trip back home
When I happened to see those kids again
Wearing brand new coats
On the corner stood a kettle
And a Salvation Army band
And a proudly smiling mother

With five dollars in her hand
As she placed the money in the pot
I could hear her tell her kids,
"Don't worry boys, Santa's bringing you toys.
Let's go home, and make a list!"

I hope you get your wish, this Christmas
Whatever it may be
Perhaps a new home of your own
Good health for your family
I hope you get your wish, this Christmas
Whatever you may need
May the Lord above bless you with His love
And a gift beneath the tree

Until a Rose Never Grows Again

Three weeks until a rose never grows again
Three weeks to make her remember when
Their beautiful love was meant to be a bond unbroken
Three weeks and it'll be too late to speak
When destiny's mistake becomes complete
With words of a promise that could never be unspoken…

The story began a long time ago
Before the last year of a summer snow
When their love seemed like something from a dream
Two children with spring in their eyes
Who blossomed like roses in paradise
In a kingdom where their romance reigned supreme

But the way of the world pulled them apart
An ocean between, yet beneath the same star
As waves of time crashed upon their separate shores
But time wore her resistance thin
Like an early frost sneaking in
And misfortune sounded a somber knock upon their doors

She lost her way back to her childhood love
What time apart doesn't destroy, the distance does
And she got swept away by another man's charms
Her memories of love—stolen by a fate unkind
And now, in three short weeks of time
She'd be ever entangled in another man's arms

But the boy she forgot she loved, sailed upon a desperate sea
Just three weeks to change the course of mistaken destiny
Just three weeks to try to make her remember when
One last impassioned attempt at rekindling
The flames of their love, so desperately dwindling
Three weeks until his life with her forever ends
Three weeks until a rose never grows again….

Somewhere In Time

Somewhere in time, you already knew me
Long before the earth moved beneath our feet
Somewhere in time, I awaited a sign
A love light to shine on a dark and lonely street

For this love of ours was written in the stars
Before the oceans were filled, and the skies became blue
While the Sun was warming, and the Earth was forming
The heavens already knew the story of me and you

For love at first sight sometimes springs to life
And the forever we feel doesn't have to come from fairy tales
A happily ever after lives as the laughter between the raindrops
And the one true love survives when all else fails

Thunderbolts and lightning are striking at any moment
And all are predestined, like the world itself is designed
For this kind of love is sent from above
And the angels know that down below
Sparks will fly when stars collide

It rests in the hand of fate for souls to intertwine
Each love story, a page in the book of life
Yes, this love of ours was written in the stars
And here we lie, you and I, somewhere in time

The Ever Changing Tide

The ever-changing tides of our multicolored emotions
As bright as the bluest skies, as dark as the deepest oceans
We feel the sun and the rain, we feel the pleasure and pain
And with every passing moment, we feel the currents change…

Sometimes the laughter lasts for only a single breath
We're overflowing with joy, then suddenly, nothing's left
But in a flash of saving grace, it comes flooding back again
With the ever-changing tide that never seems to end

Sometimes a shadow of doubt creeps in from behind
And the eyes in the brightest sunrise suddenly go blind
A single drop of fear in a cup of hope and trust
Can turn a river of gold into a field of dust

Sometimes, as it quietly lurks in the silhouette of a smile
Sadness tears apart the heart of our inner child
It awakens in the darkness, when the soul is fast asleep
To pull us from the shallows, and drown us in the deep

But although our demon's daggers—deadly to the heart
Open up new wounds, and leave their jagged scars
Their unholy reign of terror will once again subside
Replaced by the emerging sun of the ever-changing tide

Tragedy's tears become a memory of yesterday's storm
And we ride the rising tide to a shore that's safe and warm
We live in the love and the laughter until the morning after
When we wait by the surging sea, while tomorrow waits to decide
For none of us ever know how the silent river will flow
On the never-ending ride of the ever-changing tide

Somewhere Between

Will the hand of fate caress us today
With a soft and tender touch?
Or will tomorrow's tragedy turn yesterday's fantasy
Into a sea of sorrow's dust?
We can never be sure which way destiny's door
Is ultimately going to swing
Will the song of the soul sound mournful and cold?
Or inspire the melodies bluebirds sing?

In the sun's golden rays, we're riding the waves
Holding the world with confident hands
But with the stroke of a knife, what was teeming with life
Becomes a forest reduced to desert sands
And kings who think karma won't blink
When it's got them in its sights
Had better look around before they come crashing down
From prosperity's glorious heights

For high in that place, that fall from grace
Gives birth to triumph's wicked shadow
So, while bathing in delight, beware of the knife
And the scars that always seem to follow…

But somewhere between nightmares and dreams
Times of too much and too little
Somewhere between the sand and the trees
Somewhere, out there in the middle
Somewhere between the wind and the breeze
Lives a breath of peace the soul can breathe
Somewhere between a grimace and a smile
The glass half empty stays full for a while
There's a reason for hope, a way to cope
Somewhere between the last and the first
There's a stillness divine, a peace of mind
Somewhere between the best and the worst

Leap of Faith

You search for the road to Solomon's mines
The lavish riches beneath desert sands
For your life's meaning between the lines
For fortunes foretold in the palms of your hands
But no one gives maps to the treasures one seeks
To the world of dreams where fantasies roam
For the spires of gold on majestic peaks
A leap of faith must bring them home

No way to that world with no words from the wise
The key to your dreams can easily get lost
Pearls of wisdom with no rhythms and rhymes
And labor that doesn't cover the cost
Unfavorable verdicts in the trials you face
Discouraging words you're persuaded to believe
But victories are born in only one place
And a leap of faith is where they're conceived

For the heart of a champion is forged in fire
You not able to fly, if you're afraid to fall
Fear of failure can't imagine or inspire
Only faith will see what doubt never saw
So, don't let your losses serve as your guide
The believer inside tells a tale of trust
Believe in that world of your beautiful mind
And let your dreams rise from the ashes and dust

For you never embody the sum of your defeats
You're not destined to stay where you have been
As long as you carry a heart that still beats
A leap of faith is where new life begins

About the Author

After decades of song writing, a lifetime's worth of emotions now pour onto this poet's pages, like literary portraits from a pen. *The Many Colors of My Heart* is a deep, rich collection of joys and sorrows, hopes and dreams, and all the shades in between.

Eddie is also a novelist. His heart-warming romance novel, *Timeless Pages,* goes hand-in-hand with his inspiring book of poetry. Together, these two books lead readers on an emotional journey where the destination is reassuring comfort and peace. Eddie will break your heart, then make it whole again with pieces of his own; and in the process, healing is bestowed upon both the reader … and the writer.

Booklist:

The Magical Town Of Freezyville
A Wish For A Christmas Fish

You can find Eddie's "Songs From the Little Room" at:
Hear Now Music Website:
https://www/eddiesullivan.hearnow.com